Love, Life, and the Cosmos: My Simple Guide to Understanding it All

Why The Universe Exists, Why You Exist And Why Your Existential Crisis Exists

Contents

Chapter 3 - Why You Exist

Chapter 4 - The Mosaic

Preface

In the Preface usually an author talks about what made him/her write a book. I'll be as honest as I can be with you.

Life is just a game, play, risk and have fun with it!

That sentence is how I live my life. I wake up and remind myself of it almost everyday. I do so because everyday worries like bills, tasks and so on, distract me from that fact. I remember walking fast down the road looking down at the pavement thinking of all the responsibilities I have. Then I saw a bird flying free and it reminded me that I can walk on the side wall, or stand on that bench, or lick that tree. I did all three and it felt great. We are free. Free to do whatever we want in this game we call life. How liberating is it. It's so easy to forget. We must consciously remind ourselves everyday. Getting out of our comfort zone helps remind us. Let's live consciously and not let life slip by while we sit back passively because we are too scared to take a risk or too worried about meaningless worries.

We are here for a very brief amount of time before going back to where we were before we were born. I don't know what my great grandfather did. The only thing I know for sure is that he had sex, otherwise I wouldn't be here. But I don't know who he liked, how he flirted, what his hobbies were, if he liked avocados or not. I know nothing. It will be the same with me in one or two generations so.. F*ck it.. If you want to tell that girl/boy that you like her/him. Do it! If you want to quit your job. Do it! If you want to start that business. Do it!! If all your life you have searched for answers and eventually got some and got so excited that you wanted to write a book about it called Love, Life and the Cosmos despite getting a C in english. Just do it! And that pretty much sums up why I did it.

So the short answer is I wrote it because I realised that I don't know anything about my Great Grandfather.

Remember to go ahead and play the game! take the risk! Lick a tree! Get uncomfortable! Because if you don't, are you even living?

Introduction:

Disclaimer. This book is riddled with horrible analogies, cringy lame jokes and weird-ass metaphors. Okay, thank you, please proceed.

In the beginning, there was only the Universe, a vast and empty space just begging to be filled with something interesting. So the Universe decided to create some matter and see what would happen. It was a big experiment, and no one knew how it would turn out. At first, the Universe just made some simple stuff like hydrogen and helium. But then, it got a little more creative and started making heavier elements like carbon and oxygen. These elements were essential because they would eventually be used to make life. The Universe was not disappointed but excited to see what would happen next. Over billions of years, life arose on one of the Universe's planets, Earth. At first, it was just simple microorganisms, but eventually, more complex organisms evolved, like plants and animals. However, the best part was when humans showed up. They were intelligent, sexy, and had a knack for getting into trouble.

They evolved a heightened sense of curiosity and the desire to seek patterns which became the main differentiators between them and the rest of the animal kingdom. They explored the planet, built incredible societies, and even sent spacecraft to other planets and moons. Today, the Universe is still watching humanity with amazement and sometimes perhaps bewitchment, waiting to see when they will self-destruct.

These two heightened senses have caused humans to start questioning everything. At first, it was simple, like 'where is my cave'? Or 'where is the food at'? But eventually, when all basic questions were answered, humans attempted to make sense of the more fundamental questions that have puzzled them for centuries, like 'why do we have to pay so much for avocados'? 'What is the nature of reality?' 'Is it all just a dream?', 'What is the purpose of life?', 'Is there a God or higher power?' How do I get out of the friend zone?

Those were some of the most challenging questions to be asked. Imagine being the first person to ask them. Throughout history, humans have grappled with existential questions and crises in various ways. Some people have turned to religion and spirituality for answers, seeking guidance and meaning in the teachings and practices of their faith. Some have turned to philosophy and science, using reason and evidence to try understanding the nature of reality and our place in it.

Others have found solace in art, literature, and other forms of creative expression, which can provide a way to explore and express complex emotions and ideas.

In this book, I give a unique perspective because, as is often the case, the truth always lies somewhere in the middle.

Join me as we explore the origins of the Universe and life itself. Along the way, in these pages, we will embark on a journey through the absurdity of it all, from the Big Bang to the possible futures that lie ahead, which, as far as we can tell, are all pretty bleak. However, do not worry; there is a silver lining, and you won't be here for it. OR WILL YOU? Stick around to find out!

This will become more than just a tour of the cosmos if you do. I promise it will also be a journey through the human condition.

Through a blend of scientific exploration and philosophical contemplation, we will explore how the Universe and our humanity intersect. We will explore how our understanding of the cosmos and evolution shapes our understanding of ourselves and our place in the Universe.

So come along with me as we explore the Universe, Evolution, and Existential Crisis. Who knows what revelations and insights we may discover along the way? Just endure with my analogies and sense of humour (developed by evolution, I am sure) and get some tea prepared, or maybe a bottle of whiskey or two.

Chapter 1

- What The F*ck Is Going On? -

Introduction

trigger warning for a cheeky panic attack

I step into the warm bath that I pre-made just for myself. I had a great day and wanted to sit and soak that booty for a couple of hours while watching tik tok videos of cute cats or avocados. As I'm there, my wifi suddenly disconnects, but the bath is too warm and cosy for me to get up and check on it. I am now alone with the scariest thing ever, my thoughts. As they drift away, they eventually wander to a dangerous place. The question place. Inevitably my thoughts finally reach the 'what happens when I die' question. I suddenly have a feeling of dread washing over me. I realise that I have no idea if anything in my life is real or if there is anything beyond death. The thoughts start racing through my head, making it hard to focus on anything. My heart starts pounding in my chest, and I can feel my hands beginning to shake. I feel like the room is spinning around me, and I can't catch my breath. I have a sense of impending doom, and I can't shake the feeling that something terrible is about to happen. My chest feels tight, and I can feel my sexy muscles tensing up. I am struggling to stay in control as the panic takes over. I don't know how much longer I can take this overwhelming feeling of anxiety.

As the panic rises, I feel like I am losing my grip on reality. My thoughts are jumbled, and I can't seem to focus on anything. I feel like I am on the verge of a complete breakdown. The anxiety consumes me; I feel helpless and alone, trapped in this never-ending cycle of panic and fear.

Ok, I may have gone overboard with this, but it can be like that sometimes. I used to go through this like once a month. You probably weren't watching avocado videos, but you probably experienced something like this to some extent. It's the fight or flight response and can be f*cking intense. It's profoundly both you and me, and it has to be dealt with.

In this chapter, I briefly explain why this happens, my first existential crisis and a few potential solutions.

The First Moment

This book was inspired by three legendary moments that marked my adult life. The first moment took place when I had just turned 13. The second and third moments are in the fourth chapter. You'll have to make it there to find out what they are.

I was in the middle of a football game when I noticed a little white tooth on the side of the field. I immediately put aside my goalkeeper duties, rushed to it, and started digging a hole because I was good at prioritizing. I remember it as if it were yesterday.

I mean, what's more important: trying to stop the opposing team from scoring or digging up a dinosaur and winning a Nobel Prize? At least, that's what my thought process was. So I removed my gloves and started digging with my bare hands. The more I dug, the more bones I found.

I couldn't contain myself. I was tearing up, smiling and digging.

A doodle of a 13 year old me thinking i'm about to win a nobel prize.

It was all great until I heard a loud scream, at which point I turned around and noticed the enemy team had scored and eventually won the finals. That moment marked the beginning of my curiosity and my bullying, and the end of my football career. After I finished fighting a losing argument trying to explain to my classmates why digging a hole was more critical than guarding a net, I took the bones home for some serious scientific experiments and testing. After pulling my first of many-nighters studying bones using dial-up internet and some stolen books on veterinary anatomy, I finally realised it was a dead cat.

Upon this realisation, I left the house to go to my self-built Security Cave in the field nearby. I sat there holding and staring at the bones. I asked how these bones came to be? Then my focus shifted to my hand. How did my hand come to be? What the heck is it even? Then I turned my head to look at the night sky, which was starting to grow brighter. I could barely see a few stars, but that was enough to trigger the next question, where did all this come from? I literally realised that I had no clue about anything. It's as if I have been asleep for the first 13 years of my life and then suddenly woke up and realised that I have no idea what is happening. My heart started beating faster. I started sweating. My jaw clenched. And eventually, I let out a cute fart.

Obviously, that's just how I personally process stressful emotions. That is the story of my very first existential crisis.

Why Your Existential Crisis Exists

The desire for control is a natural part of the human experience and evolved as a survival mechanism. In our ancestral environment, controlling our environment and resources was essential for survival. For example, being able to control fire allowed our ancestors to cook food, stay warm, and protect themselves from predators. Similarly, managing resources such as food and water was essential for survival and reproduction.

In modern times, the desire for control is still an essential part of our psychological makeup. It gives us a sense of agency and purpose, as we feel we can shape our own lives and circumstances. It can also provide a sense of security and confidence, as we feel that we have the power to influence the outcomes of situations.

Back when I lived in Prague, I would always walk the same road to get to my university. Before I reached the building, I would always have to cross the same road. I would always get there, push the little button that makes the traffic lights turn red and cross. One day though, I had stayed awake trying to study a year's worth of Physiology in one single night. I probably went through a litre of coffee. I was buzzing. I left the house to get to uni, but I forgot to push the button this time. Until today I'm not sure if it's because I was tired or secretly wishing to get hit by a bus and skip the exam. Anyway, the point is that I noticed the traffic light still turned red without me. It made no difference if I pushed it or not. After looking into it, my professor told me that the buttons' only actual function is to give citizens a sense of control. That button is literally just a button. That is how much people crave a sense of control.

Lack of control breeds fear and uncertainty, and unless you're Zuckerburg, we humans don't like uncertainty. It all goes back to our ancestors and their love of being control freaks. You see, those early humans who were able to predict and prepare for potential dangers and challenges were more likely to survive and reproduce, passing on their genes (and their love of control) to future generations. We're a bunch of descendants of control freaks who were good at preparing for the worst.

So in that state, uncertainty pops up. Humans tend to feel uncomfortable with uncertainty because it can bring feelings of fear and anxiety. When we encounter uncertainty, our brains may go into "fight or flight" mode and try to convince us that the world is ending.

Uncertainty can breed an existential crisis when it leads to a sense of helplessness or powerlessness. An existential crisis is like a midlife crisis, but without the sports car and questionable fashion choices. During an episode, you may feel disconnected from your sense of self and your place in the world. You may question your values and beliefs and feel uncertain about the future.

The big bosses of all existential questions are 'What is the purpose of life?', 'What am I?' and 'Where am I? ' Inability to effectively answer these questions will eventually give you a lovely panic attack.

So if you noticed, there is a pattern here. It starts with evolution instilling in us a need for control. Controlling everything is impossible, so we are left with a scary lack of control. This lack of control triggers uncertainty and fear, which triggers an existential crisis that can lead to a panic attack. Just like dominos, you can stop the flow at any point before reaching the end or, in this case, the panic attack.

What Do The Experts say?

The problem of lack of control is so prominent that professionals from every part of life try to address it. Since lack of control is the starting point usually, they try to address that with their techniques.

Philosophers

One way to solve problems caused by a lack of control is to focus on what you can control. Philosophy, like Stoicism and Existentialism, can help with this. Stoicism teaches us to focus on our thoughts and actions and let go of external events. For example, if an annoying baby is sitting right next to you on a plane, crying about whatever babies cry about, a Stoic would accept that there isn't anything they can do about it and accept it. On the other hand, I would stare at the parent until they got uncomfortable and did something. But I'm not an example to follow.
Existentialism emphasizes accepting the freedom and responsibility to create your own meaning in life despite the lack of control. Both approaches can help you deal with a lack of control and prevent future problems. For example: Imagine you lose your job and are struggling to find new employment. Instead of feeling hopeless and helpless, an Existentialist would focus on the freedom and responsibility they have to create their own meaning in life.

This is the first place I went to look for answers. I turned my head to philosophy. I found it very interesting. I read a lot. I fell in love with how these people thought. They would reflect, then reflect again and then a bit more on the same thought. Everything they said was so well thought out that I could follow their thought process to the point where I could understand them. Out of all of them, I liked Jean-Paul Sartre. He came up with the concept: as long as there is no creator, you can choose your meaning. It seems straightforward now, but it wasn't back in his time. It was a revolutionary concept. Unfortunately, though, an existential crisis is not all logic. It has a lot to do with emotions too. So while I understood the reasoning, it wasn't enough. Understanding something you read doesn't necessarily mean you absorb it.

Psychologists

CBT is like the "Mighty Mind-Changer", ready to conquer the nefarious negative beliefs lurking in your brain and replace them with shiny new positive ones. On the other hand, ACT is the "Zen Master of Acceptance" that teaches you to sit with your uncomfortable thoughts, emotions and situations and learn to "be" with them, with no need to fight them.

After many people asked me, especially my ex, I went to a psychologist. While on paper, it sounded fantastic and made perfect sense, the only thing that was changing over time was my bank account balance. Don't get me wrong, psychology is vital and helps millions. It just didn't do enough for me. I have even gone to a few to make sure. The only thing genuinely helping me in those sessions was that I had someone to listen to me vent about anything and everything. I realized I could already do that for free to my unfortunate friend. He wasn't thrilled, but oh well.

Religion

Religion can provide individuals with a framework for understanding the world and one's place in it. It can also offer a sense of control through believing in a higher power or a greater plan. It provides a structure for the universe and gives you the illusion of control through the fact that you can speak with the creator himself. It also answers life's most challenging questions and comforts you in times of grief. Many religions provide practices and beliefs that can help you find inner peace and meaning, like prayer, meditation, or chanting "ohm" until you pass out from boredom.
Plus, if you're feeling lonely and want some company, many religions offer support through community activities like singing hymns in a group or gossiping.

Growing up, my mom held weekly bible study meetings with her religious friends to discuss and analyze the bible. I would always start off listening to them with an open mind hoping I could get the answers I needed, but instead, the more I heard, the more questions I had. I also found many inconsistencies and contradictions that didn't help the case. So that didn't help me either.

The night almost always ended with her friends touching my head and praying for me to see the truth finally. To be fair, I think it worked. That's why I'm writing this book; I don't think it's the truth they wanted me to see. So religion wasn't for me, either.

Superstition

I must admit that I went through this phase too. Then again, one must keep an open mind and try everything, right?

I went and had someone do the whole Tarot thing and even read zodiac signs. Let me tell you, it helped a bit. The guy doing the Tarot reading kept talking about all the good stuff that was about to happen, which definitely made me feel better. Even though it sucked when it came to impressing women, my zodiac sign felt relatable to me, and it felt good reading about its predictions. Even though I was having fun with it, and it gave me the illusion of control, my logic eventually caught up with me and didn't let me enjoy it. It kept calling out all its inconsistencies and mistakes.

So What Now?

After giving a fair trial to each of the above, I still felt it wasn't enough. That's where science came into the picture. Just like philosophy, it was so well thought out; unlike superstition and religion, it had empirical evidence, and unlike psychology, it felt like it was helping me. I became obsessed with it. I started reading Astrophysics and cosmology like there was no tomorrow. Professor Neil De Grasse Tyson and Lawrence Krauss became my idols overnight. I liked them so much that I travelled to the UK to meet Professor Lawrence Krauss, and I did. I remember telling him at the book signing that my parents wanted me to study Dentistry, but I wanted Physics. I asked what I should do, and he just wrote something in the book and gave it to me. When I opened it up, it said follow your passion. Argh, I should have listened. That happened two years before I enrolled as a dental student at uni.

Anyway, I spent many nights sitting at the dam in my town staring up at the night sky, listening to my favourite science song (Quantum World by MelodySheep google it, it's an absolute tune! While you're there, check out the rest too) and tearing up with all its beauty and grandeur. I thought I had found the solution. Science gave me a sense of connection and understanding that nothing else did. The more I learned about reality, the more connected and in control I felt. The power of the cosmic perspective truly helped me absorb what Saartre was trying to say. Knowing sets me free and minimises uncertainty as much as possible. In the following two chapters, I explain what I have learned from science and how it helped me unknowingly piece together the Mosaic of understanding.

Me and my idol Professor Krauss. I was so excited i could barely form sentences

Chapter 2

- Why The Universe Exists-

Introduction

I was 15 and super excited to get my first girlfriend... LOL, jk, I wish... I got my first telescope. I saved all my birthday money and happily gave it to this guy I found online selling his telescope second-hand. I remember when I first saw it. I let my dad deal with the guy and rushed towards it. It looked magnificent. It was a massive 10-inch Dobsonian sexy tool that I knew would propel my understanding of and curiosity towards the cosmos to another level. Size matters with telescopes (also with penises but more on that later). I waited impatiently for my dad to stop his conversation with the guy, which at this point, had somehow veered toward politics and got it home. I set up a ladder, took it to the roof, set it up and pointed it at my hot neighbour. But right after that, I pointed it at the night sky. The view was absolutely breathtaking. I saw my first star cluster - a bunch of stars gravitationally bound to one another. I saw nebulas which are these big clouds of gas. I saw the planets.

The night sky was the second most exciting thing I saw that day. It was absolutely mind-blowing. But one question remained. How in the world did all this come to be?! That question has been asked by almost every human being to walk this Earth. Theologians, philosophers and scientists have always and always will try to figure it out by proposing theories.

But in the 20th century, we made real progress in understanding the Universe's origins. With the development of modern physics and cosmology, we have been able to piece together a compelling story of how the Universe began and evolved over billions of years.
We will begin by dissecting the Big Bang theory literally fractions of seconds after its birth, explaining the most widely accepted explanation for the birth of the Universe and how a wealth of observational evidence has supported it. Come with me on this exciting journey through the vast and wondrous Universe as we seek to unravel the mysteries of its origins and discover the extraordinary story of how it all began.

A blurry picture of 15-year-old me bonding with my best friend, Mr Cosmic Peephole.

Origins Of The Universe

Let's start right at the beginning. Actually, before the beginning. Right before the Big Bang took place. Before we start our timeline, though, of all the significant events that led to the Universe's current state, I'd like to ensure that we are all on board with a few definitions and concepts.

First, we can start with the 4 fundamental forces that govern everything. These are the backbone of our entire Universe. All rules or laws can be broken except these ones.

The strong nuclear force: This force is like the "big, burly brother" of the Universe, which holds the protons and neutrons together in the nucleus, despite their positive charges typically causing them to repel each other, just like my parents. This force is responsible for the interaction between subatomic particles within the nucleus of an atom. It is the strongest of the four fundamental forces, and it acts over a concise range. Without the strong nuclear force, the nucleus would fall apart faster than a cheap suit at a wedding.

The weak nuclear force: This force is like the "sneaky little brother" of the Universe - it's not as strong as the strong nuclear force, but it can still cause some trouble. It's responsible for certain types of radioactive decay, such as beta decay, which is a nuisance. As its name suggests, it is weaker than the strong nuclear force and acts over a slightly longer range. The weak nuclear force transforms subatomic particles, such as a neutron, into a proton and an electron. It is also responsible for the process of nuclear fusion, which occurs in the cores of stars and is the source of energy for the Sun and other stars.

The electromagnetic force: Ever wonder how your phone charger works? Or how can a magnet pick up paper clips? Well, it's all thanks to the mysterious and powerful force known as electromagnetism. You see, everything in the Universe is made up of tiny particles called atoms, and these atoms have something called electrons whizzing around their nucleus. And it just so happens that these electrons have a love-hate relationship with each other. Sometimes they love each other and want to cuddle up close, but other times they hate each other and want to keep their distance. Can you relate? I hope not because that shit is toxic. This delicate balance of electric and magnetic fields allows all sorts of cool things to happen.

Side story, the Van Der Graff generator is the classic science class experiment used to demonstrate static electricity for which the electromagnetic force is responsible. It's when kids touch a ball that has been charged, and all their hair stands up. Well, I decided to

26

build one when I was 16. Long story short, I electrocuted my cat. It survived it, though, and the generator worked. Contrary to my cat's beliefs, I see this as an absolute win.

The gravitational force: This force is like the "glue" that holds the Universe together - it's what keeps the Earth orbiting around the Sun, what keeps you from floating off into space, and what keeps me from going onto aeroplanes. Without the gravitational force, the Universe would be like a giant game of cosmic billiards, with everything flying off in random directions. This force is responsible for the attractive force between masses. It is the weakest of the four fundamental forces and acts over an infinite range. It is also responsible for the curvature of spacetime, which is the phenomenon that allows massive objects, such as the Earth, to bend the path of light.

Okay, now that we've got the gist, we can start the journey. There are three main prevailing hypotheses about how the Universe began. At this point, you gotta take your pick.

One states that there's this thing called quantum fluctuations, which is a fancy way of saying that subatomic particles are wiggly and unpredictable. These wiggly little guys can sometimes cause some big ripples in the fabric of the Universe. Or so girls keep telling me. They can create particles out of thin air and even create new UNIVERSES. I mean, talk about being productive! These quantum fluctuations are basically the ultimate multitaskers. They're like, "Hey, I'm just going to take a quick break from wiggling and create a new reality while I'm at it."

And you know how sometimes you have a perfect hair day, and you're like, "I'm on top of the world!" Imagine having a perfect quantum fluctuation day and saying, "I just made a UNIVERSE!" That's a terrible analogy, but you get the point.

The other theory is called the Bouncing Universe theory. Imagine that the Universe is like a rubber ball. When you squeeze the ball, it becomes denser and smaller. At some point, it might become so dense and small that it "bounces" and expands again. This is like what the cosmic bounce theory suggests happened to the Universe before our current one.

According to this theory, the previous Universe was super dense and hot, like a mini black hole. Then, it collapsed in on itself and "bounced," creating the expansion that eventually led to the formation of our current Universe.

But seriously, scientists still research and debate this idea, so it still needs to be 100% understood. Far from it, but it's definitely a cool concept that could help us understand how our Universe came to be and how it continues to evolve.

The third one is that God did it.

Now let's jump into the 10 main stages that the Universe went through from its inception until today.

The singularity: This is where it all began, folks. Think of it like a crowded party where everyone was too packed to dance like the entire Universe was packed into one tiny, super hot and dense point. At this stage, the Universe was so small it couldn't even be measured, and the laws of physics were basically like, "Yeah, we don't really know what's going on here." The singularity is thought to have happened around 13.8 billion years ago, around the time Queen Elizabeth was born. Some people believe singularity was caused by the collapse of a previous Universe. In contrast, others think it was just a glitch in the vacuum of empty space (which, apparently, isn't actually empty). But at least we had the combined power of all four fundamental forces to keep us entertained.

During the Planck era, which lasted from 10^{-43} seconds to 10^{-36} seconds after the singularity. The only thing faster than that was 16-year-old me getting rejected by my first crush. The Universe was a hot, chaotic mess as if that party had gotten way out of hand. Everything was swirling around, with particles bouncing off each other left and right. It was a time when the laws of quantum mechanics ruled the roost, and energy was everything.

As the Universe cooled and expanded, it entered the grand unification era (This stage lasted from 10^{-36} seconds to 10^{-32} seconds after the singularity), which was like the morning after the wild party. The four fundamental forces of nature (gravity, electromagnetism, and the strong and weak nuclear forces) were still working together. Still, they were starting to sober up and go their separate ways. It was also during this time that the first elementary particles, like quarks and leptons, began to form, laying the foundation for all the matter in the Universe.

Next was the electroweak era (this stage lasted from 10^{-32} seconds to 10^{-12} seconds after the singularity), which was like brunch the morning after the party. The electromagnetic force and the weak nuclear force had a big falling out, and they decided to go their separate ways. However, they still had to hang out and be polite to each other. During this time, the first neutral atoms were formed, allowing light to travel freely through the Universe for the first time. As the Universe continued to cool and expand, it entered the next phase of its development: the quark-hadron era. This stage lasted from 10^{-12} seconds to 10^{-6} seconds after the singularity. This was when quarks and gluons (the particles that make up protons and neutrons) were the dominant forms of matter in the Universe. It was a time of great complexity and diversity as the Universe continued to evolve and change.

The quark-hadron era eventually ended, and the Universe entered the next phase of its development: the lepton era (This stage lasted from 10^{-6} seconds to 1 second after the singularity). This was when leptons (such as electrons) became the dominant form of matter in the Universe.

It's important to note that the first four eras all began and ended in the first second of the Universe's existence, approximately the same amount of time my dad gave me to solve a maths problem before he started throwing me around the house. The earlier the era, the more impact it had on its shape and behaviour. Like the earlier parents traumatise their child physically and/or mentally, the more messed up it will grow to be. If you bump a kid's head at 12, he might get a concussion, but if you do it when he's 2, he might always walk in circles for the rest of his life.

As the Universe continued to cool and expand, it entered the next phase of its development: the photon era. (This stage lasted from 1 second to 379,000 years after the singularity). This was when the Universe was filled with a diffuse gas of photons (particles of light) and other particles, and the temperature was too high for atoms to form. Remember when God said let there be light? Well, this is the point where He willed it into existence if you believe in theory number 3. Eventually, the photon era ended, and the Universe entered the next phase of its development: the atom's period, when the Universe is filled with neutral atoms and photons are free to roam around. It is a time of great complexity and diversity as stars, planets, and galaxies continue to form and evolve. Almost where we are now.

Finally, we reach the most exciting era of them all. The Stars and Galaxy Era. During this time, the Universe cooled and expanded enough for stars and galaxies to form. The temperatures during this era are estimated to be around 2.7 Kelvin. Which is the current temperature of the Universe. It translates to -270.45 °C. Almost colder than my ex-girlfriend. Almost.

Origins of Stars

Stars are giant balls of gas and dust held together by their gravity, like giant celestial meatballs. They produce light and energy through nuclear fusion, a giant cosmic microwave oven that cooks the hydrogen in their cores into helium and, eventually, other heavier elements. Smaller stars, like our Sun, can burn for billions of years before they run out of fuel and turn into a cold, lifeless rock. More prominent stars burn more quickly and may only last a few million years before they go supernova and explode in the most violent way possible.

It starts with a giant molecular cloud of gas and dust, like a cosmic culinary ingredient waiting to be turned into something delicious. As the cloud collapses under its gravity, it starts to spin and flatten into a disk-like shape, like cosmic pizza dough. This disk-like shape is called a protoplanetary disk because it's where planets are born.

As the protoplanetary disk collapses and spins, it becomes denser and hotter. Eventually, a protostar is formed at its centre. A protostar is a dense, burning ball of gas held together by its gravity and is the precursor to a fully-fledged star.

As the protostar continues to get smaller and heat up, it eventually becomes hot and dense enough to ignite nuclear fusion in its core. This process releases tremendous energy, radiated outward from the star in light and heat. This marks the beginning of the star's main-sequence phase, during which it burns hydrogen in its core to produce helium and then converts helium into heavier elements.

The same life-time of a star depends on its mass. Smaller stars, like our Sun, can burn for billions of years before running out of fuel, while more prominent stars burn more quickly and may only last for a few million years. When a star runs out of fuel, it begins to cool and contract, eventually becoming a white dwarf, a neutron star, or a black hole, depending on its mass.

But it's not just any star that forms in these clouds – the coldest clouds tend to form low-mass stars, while warmer clouds can produce stars of all masses. And most stars don't develop in isolation but as part of a group called a star cluster or stellar association.

Origins Of The Galaxies

Galaxies are like big, fancy cosmos restaurants filled with celestial meals like stars, gas, dust, and dark matter. There are different types of galaxies, spiral galaxies that look like cosmic pinwheels, elliptical galaxies that look like cosmic footballs, irregular galaxies that look like cosmic blobs and lenticular galaxies that look like lentils. The Milky Way is a barred spiral galaxy, a cosmic pinwheel with a cosmic bar stuck in the middle.

The Milky Way galaxy is a vast and mysterious place, filled with billions of stars, gas, and dust. It is a barred spiral galaxy with a central bar and four major arms containing most of its stars. The Milky Way is estimated to have a mass of about 1.5 trillion solar masses, making it one of the more massive galaxies in the Universe.

Our Sun is just one of the billions of stars that call the Milky Way home. It is located in the Orion Arm of the galaxy, a small spiral arm between the Sagittarius and Perseus Arms. The Milky Way is about 100,000 light-years in diameter, making it one of the larger galaxies in the Universe.

But how did the Milky Way come to be? Scientists believe it formed about 13.6 billion years ago, shortly after the Big Bang. The galaxy formation begins with a large cloud of gas and dust, called a molecular cloud, which collapses under its own gravity. The cloud begins to spin and flatten into a disk shape as the cloud collapses.

The material begins to clump within the disk and form small objects called protostars. These protostars are the precursors to stars and are thought to develop through the process of fragmentation within the molecular cloud. As the protostars grow, they eventually ignite and become full-fledged stars.

The process of gravitational collapse and star formation can take millions of years. As the stars form, they also heat and ionize the gas around them, creating bright nebulae, the pretty background pictures you saw. My personal favourite nebula is the eagle's nebula, as shown below. It might look modified, but I swear I didn't touch it. It is as breathtaking as in the image.

An unmodified image of the eagle nebula.

These nebulae are the birthplaces of stars and are sometimes called "stellar nurseries." Current theories suggest that there are two main types of galaxies: blue star-forming galaxies that look like spirals and are basically the party animals of the galaxy world, and red non-star-forming galaxies that look like ellipticals and

36

are more Spiral galaxies are thin, dense, and rotate quickly, while elliptical galaxies have random orbits for their stars. Many giant galaxies also have supermassive black holes at their centres, which can be millions or billions of times the mass of our Sun. These black holes are like the parents of the galaxy, keeping everything in check. Another interesting fact about galaxies is that the more metal-rich a galaxy is, the brighter it tends to be. Like how the more bling you have, the cooler you are. The first person to do this was Edwin Hubble, who devised a way to classify galaxies based on their shape and features. He called it the "tuning fork diagram" and divided galaxies into four categories: ellipticals, normal spirals, barred spirals (like our own Milky Way, which is basically the sexiest because we are in it and no one says otherwise), and irregulars (aka the rebels).

One mysterious aspect of galaxy formation is the concept of dark matter. This is a type of matter that we can't see or detect directly, but we know it exists because galaxies wouldn't behave the way they do if they didn't have a lot more mass than what we can see. Most of the mass in a galaxy is thought to be made up of dark matter. It's like the invisible glue that holds everything together.

The Milky Way is part of the Local Group of galaxies, including the Andromeda galaxy and several smaller galaxies. It is located in the outskirts of the Virgo

Supercluster, a group of galaxies that contains thousands of individual galaxies.

The Milky Way is thought to have a supermassive black hole at its centre, with a mass of about 4 million solar masses. This black hole is surrounded by a region of intense radiation, and high-energy particles called the accretion disk. The accretion disk is fed by a steady stream of gas and dust that falls into the black hole.
The Milky Way is also surrounded by a halo of dark matter. This mysterious and invisible substance makes up about 85% of the galaxy's mass. Despite its name, dark matter does not actually emit or absorb light and is, therefore, invisible to telescopes. However, scientists have inferred its existence based on how it influences the movement of stars and galaxies.

The Milky Way is visible from Earth as a faint band of light in the night sky, which is why it is called the "Milky Way." From our perspective on Earth, we can see the bright stars and nebulae of the Milky Way's spiral arms, the central bar and the dark lanes of dust that obscure the light of more distant stars.

Despite its beauty and grandeur, the Milky Way is just one of the billions of galaxies in the Universe. Each galaxy is unique, with its own characteristics and features. Some galaxies are small and compact, while others are vast and sprawling. Some are spiral galaxies, like the Milky Way, while others are elliptical or irregular.

The study of galaxies, and the Milky Way, is a fascinating and rapidly evolving field of astronomy. As we continue to explore the cosmos and learn more about the nature of the Universe, we will undoubtedly uncover even more mysteries and wonders about the galaxy we call home.

Origins Of The Planets

The process of planet formation begins with, you guessed it! The collapse of a cloud of interstellar gas and dust. The cloud begins to spin and flatten into a disk shape as the cloud collapses. This disk is called a protoplanetary disk composed of gas, dust, and ice particles. Yes, it's pretty much the same idea over and over.

The protoplanetary disk is a dynamic environment, with material constantly moving and interacting. As the disk cools, dust and ice particles stick together, forming small objects called planetesimals. These planetesimals can range from a few centimetres to a few kilometres across.

The formation of planetesimals is thought to be aided by ice in the protoplanetary disk. Ice is more likely to stick to other particles, allowing them to clump together and form larger objects. The presence of ice in the protoplanetary disk can also lead to the formation of "pebble clouds," which are regions of the disk where small particles (pebbles) are tightly packed together. These pebble clouds are thought to be an essential step in the formation of planetesimals and planets.

As the planetesimals collide and merge, they form larger and larger objects. The type of planet that forms depends on the location within the protoplanetary disk. Closer to the star, where it is hotter, planets tend to be smaller and made of rock and metal. Farther away from the star, where it is cooler, planets tend to be larger and made up of ice and gas.

The process of planet formation can take millions of years to complete. During this time, the protoplanetary disk may also contain gas, which can be accreted by the forming planets. This gas can make up a significant portion of the mass of the planets, particularly in the outer solar system, where the planets are more distant from the Sun and, therefore, cooler.

Not all planetesimals end up forming planets. Some may be ejected from the system, while others may become asteroids or comets. The leftover planetesimals and other debris in the protoplanetary disk can also collide with the forming planets, potentially altering their orbits or even causing them to break apart.

In addition to planetesimal formation and growth, several other mechanisms can play a role in forming planets. One such mechanism is gravitational instability, in which the protoplanetary disk becomes unstable and collapses directly into a planetary object. This process is thought to be responsible for forming massive planets, such as Jupiter and Saturn, in the early solar system.

Another mechanism is the "core accretion" model. A rocky core forms around a star and then accretes a gaseous atmosphere to become a gas-giant planet. This process is thought to be responsible for creating the gas giant planets in our solar system and exoplanets – planets that orbit stars outside our solar system.

So, have you ever wondered where the Earth and Moon came from? It's a mystery that has puzzled scientists for centuries, but we've finally figured it out. It all starts with a collapsing cloud of interstellar gas and dust...LOL jk, I'm not going through that again; let's skip this.

Okay, so it's 4.5 billion years ago, shortly after our Solar system was formed. Imagine a young Earth just starting out in the solar system. It's a rocky little cute planet with a thick atmosphere and a molten surface. But something's not quite right. It's missing something... something important. And then, out of nowhere, BOOM! A Mars-sized object called Theia smacks into the Earth and blasts a massive chunk of the planet's mantle and crust into orbit.

The debris swirls around the Earth until it finally comes together and forms the Moon. And just like that, the Earth has a Moon! Hooray!

This seems like a stretch, but it's actually the most widely accepted theory for the formation of the Earth and Moon. There's evidence to support it, like that the Moon is made up of the same types of rock as the Earth's mantle and that the Moon's orbit is tilted relative to the Earth's orbit around the Sun. So it's not just a wild theory – it's actually backed up by science!

I doodled the earth split into two by Theia

By now, you should have a pretty good understanding of how the Universe got to the point it is now. We went through the ten main phases the Universe has been through. It's difficult to say what comes from here on. Of Course, this would only stop physicists from coming up with hypotheses and theories. Following are three widely accepted ones that try to predict the future of our Universe.

First, we have the Heat Death scenario (also known as the Big Chill or Big Freeze). This is the ultimate downer of a future where everything just stops. The expansion of the Universe will have spread everything so thin that there won't be enough leftover goop to form new stars or galaxies. It'll be like the Universe's retirement party, except no one will be there to enjoy it. It sounds sad, but it's relatively peaceful.

Next up, we have the Big Crunch. This is the polar opposite of Heat Death - instead of everything spreading out, everything collapses back in on itself. As it turns out, the gravitational attraction of all the matter in the Universe might eventually be strong enough to overcome the expansion. And so, the Universe will start contracting, like a giant cosmic accordion. Ultimately, it will all collapse into a singularity, just like the beginning of the Big Bang. It's a do-over but on a cosmic scale.

Finally, we have the Bubble Universe scenario. This is where things get weird. The expansion of the Universe continues as usual. Still, new Universes form within it, like bubbles in a giant cosmic glass of soda. Each of these Universes could have its unique physical properties and laws of physics. It's like a cosmic Russian nesting doll, but instead of dolls, it's Universes. How cool is that? The Universe will continue to expand, but in a more complex and multifaceted way, with different regions of the Universe potentially evolving independently. Who knows what kind of crazy stuff is happening in those other Universes? Only time (and maybe a mighty telescope) will tell."

What does this mean for us?

The Cosmic Perspective

Let's pretend you're a proton whizzing around in a hot and dense early Universe. As the Universe started to cool down about 380 000 years after the big bang, you get your first electron and form a cute helium atom together. This happens to almost all your friends too. So a bunch of helium starters forming anywhere you look. Eventually, you all start getting attracted to each other thanks to gravity, slowly getting closer and closer, heating up. It starts getting so hot that you finally bump into one of your friends with just enough speed and energy to fuse with them. You both combine into a Hydrogen atom. This is the process of fusion, as described before. And just like that, a star is ignited. You then keep bumping into more and more atoms, slowly transforming into different types of atoms. Eventually, the star dies and explodes, scattering all of you and your friends into the galaxy.

So at the moment, you are a carbon atom that just exploded into space at insane speeds in the Universe's most violent explosions. But gravity doesn't let you get too far. It again starts pulling you and your buddies back, but this time instead of forming a star, you create a planet. A planet filled with all the ingredients for life itself, such as carbon, oxygen, and nitrogen. Eventually, you find yourself and your buddies to be the building blocks of everything, including life.

You are a cosmic masterpiece, made up of trillions of atoms with a history as vast and awe-inspiring as the Universe itself. Each atom has journeyed through the most explosive events in existence. Now they come together to form you - a being with unimaginable potential, strength and a cute butt.

Look at your hand - it is a canvas of stardust, representing the infinite night sky. We are all connected at the most fundamental level, and every one of us is a unique expression of the Universe in human form.
At this moment, you are a way for the Universe to be self-aware, experiencing itself through your thoughts, actions, and experiences. You are what the Universe is doing now in space and time. Next time you look at the night sky, remember you are connected to what you see at the atomic level.

All of this helped me add some tiles to the mosaic I was trying to build. It was liberating to an extent. I don't know what will happen if this doesn't give you a sense of connectedness. I felt one with everything. Everything.

Is your **existential** crisis over now? For me, it still wasn't. There was still something missing.

Chapter 3

- Why You Exist -

Introduction

The origins of life and the process of evolution by natural selection are two of the most awe-inspiring and profound mysteries of the natural world. From the earliest single-celled organisms to the diverse species we see today, life on Earth has undergone an incredible journey of adaptation and change. We will consider the complex interplay between evolution and other factors that shape life on our planet, including genetics, ecology, and the role of chance.

But how did matter come to life? What has driven the evolution of life over billions of years? Why do we fall in love? What makes a cake so good? Why do we have the biggest penis-to-body ratio? Why do we behave how we behave? Even though all these questions seem unrelated, they can all be answered through the theory of evolution. The more we understand it, the more we can understand why we act and are the way we are. These questions have titillated the most extraordinary minds throughout history. They continue to be at the forefront of scientific research today.

Seriously though, who wouldn't want to know how we went from a bunch of squiggly blobs floating around in the primordial soup to, well, you? The complex, cool, trendy and sexy being that you are today?

Let us be awed and inspired by the grandeur and complexity of the natural world and marvel at the incredible journey of life on this pretty planet.

Origins

Human evolution is the process by which humans went from being a bunch of hairy, banana-munching apes to the sophisticated (well, mostly) beings we are today. It's a long and bumpy road that took us from swinging in the trees to swiping on dating apps, and it's a journey that still needs to be finished.

Our recent early ancestors were small, apelike creatures that lived in trees and spent most of their time trying to avoid being eaten by giant predators. But as the world changed, these early humans had to adapt to survive.

One essential adaptation was the development of bipedalism, or the ability to walk on two legs. This allowed our ancestors to stand upright, which made it easier for them to see danger coming and also made them look more attractive to the opposite sex as all the reproductive organs were on display.

As humans evolved, they developed larger brains and more advanced tools and technologies. This allowed them to communicate with each other using language and to work together to solve problems and accomplish tasks (like inventing the wheel or coming up with new and creative ways to procrastinate)

Once again. Let's go back to just before the beginning.. Way back. Before the matter was even alive.

The question of how life began on Earth is one of the natural world's oldest and most enduring mysteries. From the earliest philosophers who proposed that life arose spontaneously from non-living matter to modern scientists searching for clues in the molecular structure of living cells, we have always been captivated by the question of where we came from and how we evolved. We will explore the theories and evidence surrounding the origins of life on Earth and consider the various factors that may have played a role in the emergence of the first living organisms.

One of the earliest theories about the origins of life was the concept of spontaneous generation, which held that life could arise spontaneously from non-living matter. This idea was supported by the experiments and observations that living things appeared suddenly in certain conditions, such as maggots appearing in rotting meat. I think my university roommate really liked experimenting this way. He would leave food lying around and would refuse to clean up until it started moving. Aaaanyway, this theory was eventually debunked by the experiments of Louis Pasteur, who showed that living things could only come from other things. Pasteur's experiment involved sealing a flask of broth and boiling it to kill any potential contaminants. He found that no new life forms appeared in the flask, despite the favorable conditions for growth, leading him to conclude that life could only come from other living things. It seems basic, but for his time, this was big science.

The concept of the primordial soup is a widely accepted theory about the origins of life on Earth. According to this theory, life arose through chemical reactions in a mixture of water, gasses, and organic molecules that may have existed on early Earth. The conditions on early Earth were essential to forming complex organic molecules, such as amino acids, sugars, and nucleotides, through the action of lightning, UV radiation, and other energy sources. These molecules then reacted with each other to form more complex structures, eventually giving rise to the first living cells.

The idea of the primordial soup was first proposed by the Russian scientist Alexander Oparin in the 1920s and has since been supported by a wealth of scientific evidence. Many of the building blocks of life, such as amino acids and sugars, can be formed under laboratory conditions that simulate the conditions that may have existed on early Earth. For example, amino acids can be synthesized from simple gasses through the action of UV radiation or electrical discharge, and sugars can be formed through the reaction of simple organic molecules under certain conditions. Additionally, scientists have been able to recreate some of the chemical reactions that may have occurred in the primordial soup, such as the formation of RNA. This molecule plays a central role in storing and expressing genetic information.

The early Earth was a very different place than today, with a much hotter and more volatile atmosphere. The atmosphere was composed of gasses such as methane, ammonia, and water vapor, which are conducive to forming complex organic molecules. In other words, the early Earth was basically a giant fart in a jar. But fear not, dear reader! This smelly concoction eventually led to the emergence of life on our planet.

Despite the progress in understanding the chemistry of the primordial soup, there are still many mysteries surrounding the emergence of the first living cells. For example, scientists are still trying to understand how the first cells formed and what conditions were necessary for their emergence. Additionally, the question of how life first arose remains one of the great unsolved mysteries of science. We will likely continue to make new discoveries and revise our understanding of the origins of life as we learn more about the complexity and diversity of life on Earth. But one thing is for sure: the primordial soup is a soup-er theory (apologies for that) about the origins of life on our planet. So grab a spoon and dig in. (Not sorry for that one)

Another well-established hypothesis is the concept of Panspermia. Panspermia is the wild idea that life on Earth, or anywhere else for that matter, may have been brought to us by little space-traveling microbes hitching a ride, meteorites, or interplanetary dust particles (IDPs). Think of it like a cosmic game of "mail-a-microbe."

Several experiments have shown that certain types of microorganisms, like bacteria, can withstand the extreme conditions of space. This means that they could potentially survive a trip through the vast emptiness of the Universe and make it to a new home.

One of the primary pieces of evidence for the possibility of Panspermia is the discovery of microfossils in meteorites that have fallen to Earth. These microfossils are thought to be remnants of ancient microbial life, and their presence in meteorites suggests that it may be possible for microorganisms to survive the harsh conditions of space and be transported from one planet to another.

In addition to discovering microfossils in meteorites, there have also been several other lines of evidence supporting the idea of panspermia. For example, some researchers have suggested that microorganisms could survive the harsh conditions of space by hunkering down in a dormant state, like a spore or cyst. Others have proposed that life could be encased in a protective layer of ice, like a cosmic popsicle, to survive the journey. This suggests that it may be possible for microorganisms to survive the journey through space and be transported to other planets or moons.

My doodle of a microbe on a space rock on its way to fertilize an entire planet

That's why when I see a shooting star, I make sure no one can see me and I give it a small wave because it could be a tiny, space-faring organism saying hello (or goodbye) to its home planet. Or, you know, it could just be a rock. Either way, it's a pretty cool thought! Think about it, If it's true, then we could all be aliens (in the most literal sense of the word).

Another possible hypothesis that is also widely accepted is that God did it.

Evolution By Natural Selection
Evolution by natural selection is a powerful and fundamental process that has shaped the diversity of life on Earth. It is a testament to the resilience and adaptability of life, as organisms have been able to evolve and survive in a wide range of environments over billions of years.
The process of natural selection involves three key factors: variation, inheritance, and selection.

1. **Variation**: All populations of organisms exhibit variation in their characteristics, such as size, shape, color, and behavior. For example, a population of birds may exhibit variation in the color of their feathers, with some individuals having brown feathers and others having black feathers. This variation is due to the combination of different genes inherited from their parents, as well as the influence of environmental factors.

2. **Inheritance**: When organisms reproduce, they pass on their inherited traits to their offspring.

These traits are determined by the genes in the organism's DNA, passed on from generation to generation. For example, a bird with brown feathers may pass on the gene for brown feathers to its offspring, resulting in more individuals with brown feathers in the next generation.

3. **Selection**: The environment plays a crucial role in natural selection, as it determines which traits are advantageous or disadvantageous for an organism to have.

I'll attempt to give one example of it. Imagine a group of clumsy gazelles on the African savanna, stumbling and tripping all over the place as they try to escape predators. "Oh no, not another lion!" they exclaim as they frantically try to run away. But wait, there's hope! Some of the gazelles have longer legs than others, and they can easily outrun the lion. "Phew, that was close!" they say, panting and sweating. "But hey, at least we have these super-long legs to thank for our survival!"
Over time, the gazelles with longer legs are more likely to survive and reproduce, passing on their long-legged genes to their offspring. Meanwhile, the poor short-legged gazelles are constantly being eaten by lions and other predators, so their genes aren't passed on to the next generation. As a result, the population of

gazelles evolves to have longer and longer legs, all thanks to natural selection.

Now the gazelles can outrun any predator that comes their way, and they have a grand old time bounding across the savanna. "Look at us go!" they exclaim. "We've evolved into the ultimate running machine! Thanks, natural selection!"

This illustrates how the interaction of variation, inheritance, and selection can lead to changes in a population over time. The variation, in this case, is that some gazelles would have short legs, whereas others have long ones. The inheritance is the fact that the traits for long and short legs are passed onto offspring. The selection pressure is added by the environment. In this case, the lions.

This is how evolution by natural selection allows organisms to adapt and thrive in changing and challenging environments. It is a reminder of the incredible capacity of life to evolve and overcome new challenges, and it is a source of inspiration for the ongoing pursuit of scientific understanding and progress.

Here i doodled an accurate depiction of a gazelle escaping from a vicious tiger because of its long legs

Let's make this personal, very personal :D

We could look at any physical or behavioral characteristic of any animal, which can very likely be explained by the simple process of natural selection. That would mean that for humans, at least a lot of the characteristics males have been ones that women found attractive. Otherwise, they would simply not reproduce with the specific primate. Women are the ones that bear the babies; they are also the gatekeepers and evolutionary path-makers for us all. Whichever characteristic females select will become the common characteristic in just a few generations. If you're a dude reading this, then what I'm saying is that me and you are basically products designed and produced by women.

It's no secret that primates have a strong sex drive, but did you know that it goes back more than 60 million years? That's right, even the first primates that evolved during the late Mesozoic era were getting it on. And it's not just about reproduction – many primate sexes have been motivated by females choosing the best mates.
But what makes a male primate stand out from the rest? Well, according to research, it's all about size and satisfaction. Female primates can have multiple orgasms, and it's thought that ancient hominid females sought out males who could give them the best sexual experience. This led to the evolution of larger, more flexible penises through a process called sexual selection.

Today, the average erect gorilla penis is a measly 3.18 cm, while chimpanzees and bonobos average around 7.62 cm. On the other hand, humans have a much more impressive average of 12.7 cm.
The larger size of the human penis suggests that our ancestors needed to sexually satisfy females with a choice in their partners. It is believed that ancestral

females had more sexual freedom than is typically allowed in Western cultures today. There may have been a period of matriarchy where females had more control over choosing partners.

Sometimes I like to remind myself of the fact that even the mighty gorillas can't compete with the human penis in size and flexibility. We have women to thank for the evolution of our impressive human package. Just try not to let it go to your head – it's not all about the size of your junk; there's more to a successful relationship than that, like lots of and lots of money.

In this example, the variation in the different lengths of penises, the inheritance is the fact that these differences are packed into genes ready to be passed on, and the selection pressure is women!

Macroevolution vs Microevolution

Macroevolution refers to large-scale evolutionary changes resulting in new species' emergence. These changes typically involve significant changes in the anatomy and physiology of the organisms. They may include the development of new traits or the loss of existing attributes.

Macroevolution is like the blockbuster movie of evolution - it's the grand, sweeping story of how one species transforms into another over millions of years.

Examples of macroevolution include the evolution of birds from reptiles, the evolution of whales from land-dwelling mammals, and the evolution of humans from primates. These changes involve significant differences in the anatomy and physiology of the organisms. They are thought to have occurred over millions of years.

On the other hand, microevolution is more like a short film at a film festival - it's the small-scale stuff that happens within a single species or population. Microevolutionary changes may include the development of new characteristics or the loss of existing features. These changes can result from natural selection, mutation, or other evolutionary mechanisms. They may involve changes in the frequency of certain traits within a population. Still, they do not necessarily result in the emergence of new species.

These changes typically involve small changes in the genetic makeup of the organisms. They may occur over a relatively short time frame, such as within a single generation. Examples of microevolution include the evolution of antibiotic resistance in bacteria, the evolution of drug-resistant viruses, and the evolution of insect resistance to pesticides (which means they no longer get killed when exposed to our medicines).

Overall, macroevolution and microevolution are driven by the same underlying processes, such as natural selection and mutation. However, they differ in the scale of the changes they involve and the time frame over which they occur. Macroevolutionary changes can occur over millions of years, while microevolutionary changes may occur. My mother would say microevolution is me finally doing laundry. In contrast, macroevolution is me getting a job and becoming a fully-fledged, productive member of society.

Let's travel back to the first organism. The real OG!

So, you cute multicellular apex predator of a human, let's get down to the juicy stuff. Which is a brief overview of the timeline from the first organism to today.

The mighty prokaryotic cell was the first creature to emerge from the primordial soup. This single-celled organism refused to be contained by the confines of a nucleus or other boring organelles. These cells are believed to have evolved a staggering 3.5 billion years ago. They are known for their impressive simplicity, petite size, and lightning-fast reproductive rate. But don't let their cute appearance fool you - prokaryotic cells can survive in the most extreme environments, including scorching temperatures, high levels of radiation, and even extremely salty water.

Prokaryotes are divided into two main categories: the mighty bacteria and the mysterious archaea. Bacteria can be found virtually everywhere on Earth, performing incredible feats, including fixing nitrogen, decomposing matter, and causing diseases because even bacteria need hobbies. Archaea, on the other hand, are found in some of the most extreme environments on the planet, such as hot springs and salt lakes, and they have evolved to thrive in these harsh conditions.

The evolution of multicellular life was a significant turning point in the history of life on Earth, allowing for the development of more complex and varied forms of life.

The evolution of multicellular life also paved the way for cells to specialize and perform specific functions within a larger organism. This process, known as cell differentiation, allows for the creation of tissues and organs, essential components for properly functioning complex organisms.

But the evolution of multicellular life didn't stop there - it also introduced the concept of sexual reproduction, allowing for greater genetic diversity and the ability to adapt to changing environments. This process involves the exchange of genetic material between two individuals, resulting in offspring with a unique blend of genes from both parents.

The simple introduction of sexual reproduction was arguably the most critical event that still dominates our everyday life. Because of it, love had to evolve. Love was a necessary evolutionary trait that had to be to make sure the parents of the offspring actually stuck around. They ensured their offspring would have anything they needed to grow up. Sex and love are the primary motivators for almost all of modern society. I mean, think about it. I don't even know you, and I feel very confident assuming that you would like to meet a cute person that would swoop you off your feet and perhaps get frisky with you. We are more similar than different because evolution has hardwired some essential software in every one of us. Sex and love are the core.

I got sidetracked, so basically, going back to the questions we asked at the beginning of this chapter, you see that they can now be answered. Why do we fall in love? Because the ones who didn't have chances are their kids died because they never cared for them. Why do we like cake? The cake is sweet, which means energy, which is essential when trying to survive. Guess what happened to the ones that didn't like sweet things. That's right.. DEATH. I'm exaggerating, but you get the point. Why do we hate heights? Because all the ones that didn't care for heights fell off. Do you see the pattern? It's fun to think about it. Even something as trivial as red lipstick can be explained with the same trail of thought. Red lips are a sign of health, but more than that, the color red is associated with arousal; both are reproduction indicators.

Our behavior and physical form is a detailed statue, sculpted and scarred by the hands of evolution. All lessons learned and mistakes made by our ancestors are chiseled right onto our DNA and, therefore, our body and mind. By studying ourselves, we can understand what selection pressures must have existed in the past.

What does all this mean to you?

Evolution is the story of how we went from being a bunch of single-celled organisms living in the primordial soup to the complex and diverse array of species we have today.

But it's not just about the evolution of humans - it's about the evolution of every living thing on Earth. So when you think about it, that means even your beloved houseplant is related to you. It may seem like it's just sitting there minding its own business. Still, deep down, it's got some serious evolutionary history. Fun fact, we share 60% of our DNA with avocados.

And let's not forget about our distant cousins, the animals. They're all part of the same evolutionary family tree, from the tiniest ant to the mightiest elephant. So next time you see a creature, just remember: you're not so different after all. You're both just a bunch of hyper-evolved atoms trying to navigate this crazy thing called life.

So basically, that person that you kissed, yeah. They are your relatives. But so is every other living thing on this planet. It's only a matter of how distant of a relative they are. Think about it next time you're kissing someone! On a less creepy note, we are all one big ~~happy~~ family. All these answers really reduced the uncertainty I felt. Also made me feel a sense of community / family.

Is your existential crisis over now? I mean we answered a lot of questions.. Is something still missing?

Chapter 4

- The Mosaic -

The Second Moment

This Chapter instead of an introduction I would like to just dive in directly into the Second Moment.

Remember the short story at the start of the book detailing 1 of the 3 most influential moments in my life? Well, here goes the second.

As a dental student, I embarked on a journey to understand the intricate inner workings of the human body. I dedicated countless hours to studying anatomy, pouring over my atlas and memorising every detail. I was fascinated by the complexity of the human body. I spent many hours in the anatomy lab, dissecting cadavers and examining the various systems and structures up close. The experience was at times, but I was driven by a deep sense of curiosity and a desire to learn as much as possible about the human body.

But my love for anatomy wasn't the only passion that consumed me during my time as a dental student. I spent my free time reading about astronomy and astrophysics. I also developed a deep interest in the mysteries of the Universe. I was captivated by the vastness and complexity of the cosmos. I spent many late nights stargazing and trying to wrap my mind around the grandeur of it all.

As I learned about the evolution of life on Earth, I began to see the interconnectedness of all things, from the cells in our bodies to the stars in the sky. I was struck by how the forces of evolution had shaped the diversity of life on our planet and by how the same principles that governed the evolution of life could also be seen at work in the evolution of the Universe itself.

One fateful day, as I sat on my favourite bench at the top of the hill, smoking my pipe and lost in thought, I had a moment of clarity. As I looked down at my hand, I saw it not just as a simple appendage as I did when I was just 13, but as a marvel of intricate design, with veins, muscles, bones, and skin all working perfectly together in harmony. It was no longer a scary mystery to me. And when I turned my gaze upwards towards the night sky, I saw not just a collection of stars and unanswered questions but the beginning of the Universe itself. At that moment, I was filled with a sense of awe and wonder at the vastness and complexity of the world around me.

I realised that by studying the intricacies of the human body, I was gaining a deeper understanding of the world as a whole and that by exploring the mysteries of the Universe, I was gaining a deeper understanding of my place in it. As all the information and knowledge settled in my mind, I had a moment of pure euphoria. I had never felt so connected and whole with the Universe and everyone around me. Unfortunately, the feeling of euphoria quickly faded. Those facts that gave me all that sense of belonging and ecstasy are the same that abruptly triggered a little existential crisis. It wasn't the same as my first moment. It was much calmer. Once I chilled out, I remember wondering. That it was strange.

I had more information and answers than when I was 12 and had almost the same crisis. Why... it doesn't make sense.

The last ingredient

In the third chapter of this book, we delved into the concept of evolution. How it has shaped us into the complex and multifaceted beings we are today. Evolution has given us both logical and emotional traits, and it is clear that emotion has played a more significant role in shaping our behaviour and decision-making than logic. Think about it: What do we say when someone starts acting irrationally? "Oh, they must be in love." (Or, you know, have a mental disorder (often hard to distinguish between the two, heh). This demonstrates the power of emotion and how it can trump logic, reason and facts. That's how powerful it is. I'm not saying it should; I'm just pointing out that it does.

We have often used stories, myths, and metaphors throughout history to convey essential concepts and ideas. These stories were so compelling because they often blended emotion with facts, allowing our emotionally-driven brains to better understand and relate to the information being presented. Epic poems like Homer's The Iliad and The Odyssey are excellent examples of this. They aren't real. They are entirely made-up stories, but they convey a real message that would otherwise be difficult to grasp.

This emphasis on emotion may help to explain why society can sometimes seem so chaotic and unpredictable. With 8 billion people on this small, rocky planet, each with their own emotions and desires, it is no wonder that things can get a bit frisky at times.

Not all emotions, however, are born equal. The emotion that has more power over anything else, the biggest, baddest emotion of them all, is by far... *drumroll plays in the background* LOVE!! (although I must admit being hangry is a close second). The final ingredient in understanding our place in the cosmos is love and being in love. I know, I know, it's super cringy, but it's true though. I'll sound cheesy but let me explain because it's not as simple as it sounds. There are four main types of love.

First up, we have Self-love. It is another necessary type of love, and it's our love for ourselves. It's the kind of love that helps us to take care of ourselves and feel good about ourselves. It's the love that inspires us to treat ourselves to a nice meal or a spa day, and it's the love that helps us to feel confident and secure in who we are. Self-love is something that we should all strive for, even if it means indulging in the occasional self-care Netflix marathon. When was the last time you told yourself that you love yourself?

Achieving self love is not easy because we are our worst critics. Sometimes we should take a moment and appreciate ourselves. Talk to ourselves in the mirror like you're your own best friend. Go ahead and compliment that cute butt of yours. It's ok to flirt with you from time to time :) I took it a step further and even made a "self love playlist" full of songs that make me feel good about myself such as im Sexy And I Know it by LMFAO and literally any ABBA song. Perhaps though, the most important tip I have is to surround yourself with positive, supportive people who lift you up and are actually happy for your happiness.

Next we have romantic love. Being in love is like jumping into a pool of warm, gooey happiness and never wanting to leave. It's like being high on life, except the only drug you need is your significant other's presence. It has the power to turn even the most boring facts into something that's beautiful and meaningful. For example - if someone told you that "we're just a tiny, insignificant speck floating aimlessly through the vast, empty void of space until we someday drop dead," you might be tempted to curl up in a ball and cry. But if you're head over heels in love, that same statement might make you giggle and say something like, "Well, at least we have each other to keep us company on this crazy little rock yey :D". Being in love can make even the bleakest circumstances feel amusing and bearable. It's what makes us do things we never thought we would. Like writing cringy letters and going to brunch and paying 18 euros for a hard boiled egg with a dash of pesto.

Achieving this is not easy. It's actually super hard. In fact it's so hard that very few people get to experience it in the first place. Very few couples out there are actually in love. Unfortunately there is no guideline on how to do this. It just kind of happens. You can't force it. I know that timing, attraction and chemistry are important though. That's all I know. I always found it interesting how we know so much about space and nature but we still know so little about being in love.

Sometimes, being in love can start as a simple wow moment. It can happen out of nowhere. This doesn't always lead to love though. But if and when it does, it can be very powerful. I have one wow moment that I'd like to share.

There was this girl. I went out with her once and I knew I kinda liked her because I was super awkward. I remember her trying to smooth things out but I am a man of consistency and kept it awkward throughout the whole time. Anyway, after that I somehow convinced this really smart, super intuitive girl with a spectacular butt to go to a festival with me. We went to this huge festival buzzing with music, lasers and probably weed. There were a lot of security guards and they wouldn't let us get any drinks inside and as a millennial in this economy I couldn't start ordering drinks at the bar without selling an organ. So we decided to get some drinks from the local convenience store and smuggle it inside. I started pacing around trying to figure out how the heck are we going to make this happen. At that moment I turned around and saw her trying to shove the small bottle of Jägermeister under her pants. As she struggled to get that bottle to stay up there, she looked to me for some help and It struck me. The music blurred. Time slowed down. Her eyes captivated me. I saw all the little imperfections in her irises. I saw how one eyebrow was slightly misaligned with the other. She was absolutely perfect. I was blown away. She was wow!

A doodle of her proudly standing inside the festival after she smuggled it in. P.S. She is much hotter in person :3

Ok, back to our types of love. Next is platonic love, the kind of love we have for our closest friends. Platonic love is a special bond that we cherish and hold dear, even if we don't always show it with grand gestures and declarations of affection. It's the kind of love that makes us feel like we've got each other's backs no matter what. This love inspires us to go on wild adventures and have epic sleepovers, and the love helps us get through tough times.

Achieving platonic love requires spending as much time as possible with the person you want to feel platonic love for. Bonus points if you can convince them to be your Netflix-and-chill buddy (just remember, no actual chilling allowed). Communication is critical, so be sure to have deep and meaningful conversations about things like your favourite memes and whether or not pineapple belongs on pizza. It's essential to show affection by sending cute cat videos daily or surprising them with a bouquet of their least favourite flowers. Finally, respect their boundaries unless they have a weird fear of clowns. In that case, hire a clown to follow them around and constantly whisper, "I'm not scary; I promise."

Finally, there's love for one's community or, more significantly, the type of love we have for the people and causes that are important to us. It's the love that inspires us to get involved and make a difference, whether it's in our community or on a global scale. It helps us feel connected and gives us a purpose, and it's the love that drives us to be more compassionate and understanding towards others. Humans were meant to be herd animals, not solo creatures. As people, we need to feel united in working towards a common goal. People unite over a shared belief, such as religion; they also join under a common threat, such as war. Living in a world where everything is becoming more and more personal and individual is definitely making feeling a part of a community harder and harder. Religion seems to be fading, and there isn't a clear threat.

Achieving this entails finding a challenge or a problem and solving it with others who also believe it's worth solving. It could be anything. For example, if you can't find the perfect avocado at the grocery store, you could start an underground avocado-smuggling ring with like-minded individuals. In case you haven't noticed, I'm really into avocados.

So the secret ingredient, which is love, isn't that easy to acquire. It needs all of its four pillars to be there. It all starts with self-love. Without it, the other three types are almost impossible to get.

Ok, let's ground all this with a bit of science. Love has powerful psychological effects on the human mind and behaviour. It can alter our brain chemistry, releasing feel-good chemicals such as dopamine and oxytocin that can improve our mood and make us feel more connected to others. All these types of love have originated as a byproduct of the sexual revolution of species, as was explained in chapter 3. It has since become arguably the most powerful motivator in human nature, capable of even transcending death. Although we mentioned four different types of love, romantic love and being in love are arguably the most vital.

Love is so central to our existence that without it, even the most detailed explanation of the world and our place in it will still leave us feeling incomplete and unsatisfied.

It is the glue that holds everything together and allows us to form a cohesive and complete understanding of ourselves and the world around us.

So while knowledge and information are the individual mosaic tiles, which are vital, it is love that acts as the cement, filling in the gaps and bringing everything together to form a complete picture. To see the beauty in the picture, though, one must be in love.

The Third Moment

The steps that were needed for the moment to happen:

Step 1 - Drop Out

While studying dentistry, I remember everyone knew me as my fathers son. His natural successor to his dental practice. I never felt like I had my own identity. I remember doing a tooth filling as fast as I could in class just to get out of class. The professor told me I should redo it, so I did. 2 minutes later, I told him I had finished it. He checked it and once again said I should redo it. Frustrated, I sat back at my desk and looked at my classmate next to me. She was really taking her time. I whispered to her, 'hey, why are you taking so much time?' and she replied, 'I'm enjoying the process of sculpting this filling'. That's where it hit me. All of a sudden, I realised what I knew all along. Dentistry wasn't for me. I got up and left the class without saying a single word. I walked to the principal's office and asked to drop out of uni. She looked at me, shocked and asked why. I smiled and said I don't enjoy sculpting the filling and left. I wasn't so cool about it when I told my dad, though. He almost punched me through the telephone. Was horrible but that marked the first day that people started to notice me as Christos and not as 'his' son.

Step 2 - Creating my path.

I had an idea for many years but was always too scared to act upon it. Dropping out of university, though, was the push I needed since I had literally nothing to lose. When a guy reaches that point, crazy things can happen. The idea was for an app. I created my first company with my brother. That's for a whole other book, though.

Step 3 - I met a girl.

I was at the bar when I saw this beautiful girl. Absolutely gorgeous. I approached her and asked her if she liked science. She said yes, so I proposed an experiment. I told her, Instead of me flirting with her, going on dates and eventually kissing and realising we have no chemistry, why don't we kiss now? She slapped the arrogance out of me. After some of my best convincing skills and arguments, I finally got her to go out with me for a walk. Long story short, we got together, fell in love and connected on a very, very deep level.

The Actual Moment

My parents can't even be in the same room for more than 30 seconds. But my birthday was coming up, and I used those same convincing skills that I used on that girl to get my parents to both show up at the same time. It worked! My girlfriend and my cousin were there too.

Everyone gathered around me to wish me a happy birthday. As I blew the candles out, I turned to the sky to make my wish. At that moment, for the first time in my entire life. I was complete. My romantic love, the girl, was there. My platonic love, my parents and my cousin were there. My dropping out of uni was the first time I listened to what I wanted and not what others wanted for me. I prioritised myself first. Self-love was there.

And starting my own company and working on something we truly believed in that seemed to help the community and make them happy completed the love for one's community check box.

All that, mixed with the cosmic perspective, brought about unimaginable euphoria and tranquillity.

The Blend

You see, dear sexy reader, the mosaic of life must be completed in order for the picture to make sense. There are many ways to construct the mosaic. Some use religion as their base, others use philosophy etc. One thing that remains constant is the cement though. It must be love, and as we mentioned, all 4 different types of it. After trying everything else I chose science as my base. It is the most concrete base I have built and the one that gives more stability and empowers me more than anything else because of its empirical nature. It is also arguably as spiritual as anything else. As we mentioned it truly provides and proves a level of connection to your surroundings that literally reaches the atomic level.

It is unlikely that we will ever be able to fully answer all the existential questions that have kept us awake throughout history.

Picture a giant circle that represents all the stuff we humans have figured out so far. Right outside the circle is the giant abyss of the unknown. Every time we learn something new, the circle grows just a tiny bit. The bigger it gets, the more surface area it

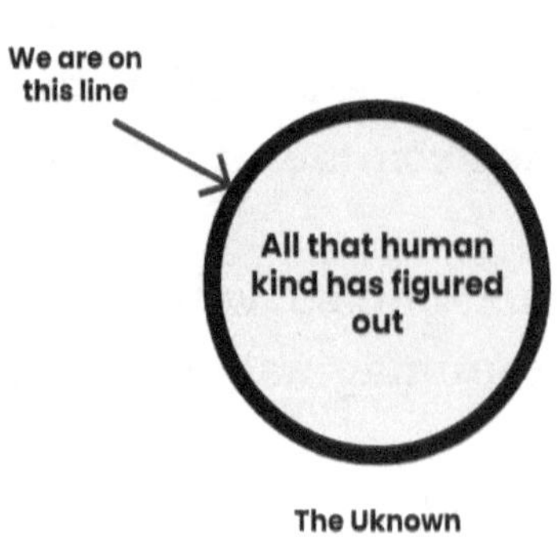

The Uknown

has, the more we are exposed to the unknown. Which just goes to show that the more we learn, the more we realise we have no idea what's going on. When I was a kid, I was worried that by the time I became a scientist, there would be nothing left to discover. But that wasn't the case. It's like an endless puzzle that just keeps growing and growing.

However, science and facts are essential for establishing a strong foundation, which was the purpose of the book's second and third chapters. This foundation helps ground us in reality as much as possible and gives us a solid base to distinguish between facts, fiction, and superstition. Science also helps us adopt a critical way of thinking, a vital tool we must use when presenting information. Without it, we are left in a confused state, vulnerable to believing anything, and in that state, one could never form The Mosaic.

Learning about the Universe and life helped me answer a lot of the questions I had and pushed uncertainty to shrink as much as it could. Love is the last punch needed to dissolve uncertainty once and for all.

Even if we could acquire all the answers, this alone would not be enough to resolve our existential crises fully. In fact, having all the answers could potentially lead to an even more profound crisis as we are forced to confront the implications of these new insights. For example imagine you knew that after death you get stuck in a small room for eternity. That is such a shitty thing to know and definitely wouldn't help out. My example was extreme but you see my point.

So facts and knowledge are essential, but the key to overcoming existential crises is not simply finding answers but cultivating a sense of love and connection with the world and people around us. When combined with a general understanding of the nature of existence, this sense of love and connection can help us navigate the complexities and uncertainties of life from a very different point of view. Ultimately, this recipe of love, facts and understanding holds power to end existential crises and help us find a sense of meaning and purpose in our lives. One that is positive, motivating and makes you eager to wake up and live your day to the fullest.

Remember, you embody the Universe's beauty, intelligence, and creativity, and we are all part of this grand cosmic tapestry. Embrace your power and potential as a cosmic being, and let your light shine brightly for all the Universe to see. We are all a big family on a rock whizzing through space. All we need is a little love and avocados :)

All of us already have a mosaic, whether we know it or not. It's needed to structure our world. Some of us are still building it, others have built it but just switched out tiles, others built it but it's super fragile and others have a literally bulletproof mosaic. A bulletproof mosaic might sound like the best option but it's not. We must always be open to looking at what other people have constructed and consider switching tiles if it makes sense to. Many times the mosaic is so vital that people define themselves with it, so it could even be dangerous to go ahead and nudge or play with it. One must take care when handling such delicate matters. We shouldnt hide our art and we must be open to having it rearranged.

It is your turn my friend, to choose your own base that inspires you and build your own mosaic consciously, tile by tile. It's a long process but it is what keeps it interesting. Don't you think?

Even though I might not know you, I Love You <3 :)

Acknowledgements

I would like to take a moment to thank my dear friend, Aletia Trakakis for helping me edit this book and all my terrible speling mistakess.

Thank you! I sincerely appreciate it!

If you would like to contact me, you can do so here: <u>christospashias6@gmail.com</u>

You can buy this book as a paperback but also as an ebook

9 789925 798001